WHO FINDS *a Wife*

A MAN'S GUIDE TO FINDING THE WOMAN & LOVE HE DESIRES

STEPHAN LABOSSIERE

He Who Finds a Wife – *A Man's Guide to Finding The Woman & Love He Desires*
Copyright ©2019 by Stephan Labossiere for Stephan Speaks, LLC
Published by Highly Favored Publishing
Second Edition: April 2019

For information, contact Highly Favored Publishing –
highlyfavoredent@gmail.com

Editor & Creative Consultant: C. Nzingha Smith

Formatting: Ya Ya Ya Creative – www.yayayacreative.com

ISBN No. 978-1-5119364-1-5

PRINTED AND BOUND IN THE UNITED STATES OF AMERICA

TABLE OF CONTENTS

INTRODUCTION

Contrary to popular belief, men get lonely too. Society likes to make it seem like men don't have feelings, and all we care about is good food and great sex. Granted, most men do love to eat well and don't mind some good bedroom loving, but there is so much more to us than that.

Most men, like most women, desire to have a special someone in their lives. These same men enjoy the stability of a committed relationship and have no problem maintaining one. Let the world tell it, and they'd have us believe that hardly any men want to get married at all.

However, this isn't true. There are plenty of men who value marriage and desire to get married; the issue they face is finding a woman they truly want to spend the rest of their lives with.

I hear men say it all the time, "It's hard to find a good woman." These men feel the *quality* of available women is rapidly declining. You too might fall under the frustrated category; due to the confusing behavior you see with the women you have come across.

Many women continuously entertain men who are no good for them and turn their backs on the men who want to love them and treat them right. This self-defeatist behavior has left plenty of men with negative feelings toward women, love, and relationships. These negative experiences have shaped the mindset of some men and caused them to point their finger and blame women as a whole for the poor state of relationships in society today.

However, what if I told you the finger needs to be pointed back at you?

If you're the guy who thinks there aren't enough good women around anymore, well think again. If struggle to attract the women you want, then I have plenty to share with you as well. I'm going to help you change your negative perception and your negative results. There still plenty of great women available. However, you have to realize and understand there are things you may be doing to hurt your chances of receiving the great woman you deserve and desire.

Don't get me wrong, I'm not saying there aren't a lot of women engaging in foolishness. I don't deny that there is an issue with women who embrace the *good for nothing* man while pushing away the man with potential, who treats her right. What I'm saying is there is more to it than that. There are certain things as a good man you can do better to avoid falling victim to always being overlooked.

However, you have to be willing to embrace the improvements that need to be made.

I grew up with my father and I love my dad, but sometimes fathers don't know how to establish a relationship with their sons that allows for open and honest communication. That being said, I wasn't taught the things I needed to know about relationships and women growing up.

Fathers often overlook the need to pass down information and enlighten their sons on what obstacles to expect in life and in love, and how to overcome them. Many times, this doesn't happen out of a lack of love, but a lack of understanding. Because the same thing happened between them and their fathers growing up or the absence thereof.

Many men didn't have fathers growing up or other men around that could be a father figure and give them guidance in life. This has created a sort of learn-as-you-go model for many men. This method of learning is less beneficial than if you're guided by wisdom and given instructions on what to do in certain situations.

It honestly doesn't matter whether or not you had a father, brother, or some other type of male figure to help you learn some of the valuable lessons needed while growing up. It's never too late to learn them.

In this book I will share with you some of the things I believe all men need to hear about manhood, life, love and relationships.

Here are a few things I want you to be mindful of while reading:

THIS BOOK ISN'T JUST ABOUT FINDING A WIFE

I know what the title says, but this isn't only about finding a woman you can spend the rest of your life with. It's as much about self-reflection and your growth as a man, as it is about finding love.

In this book you will learn more about yourself and where your focus needs to be in preparation for your wife. I'm going to give you plenty of tips to help you navigate the dating process. In addition to the tips I share, I'm also going to include information on the types of behavior you should practice, to increase your chances of attracting a great woman into your life.

I'M NOT HERE TO BASH OR JUDGE YOU

Although, I may point out flaws and patterns of negative behavior you may or may not be engaging in, don't take it as an attack or an attempt to put you down. It's being done for a purpose. I want to bring clarity and awareness to the areas that need improvement, so you can get better results in life and love.

No one is perfect. We all have to embrace correction in our lives if we truly want to see progress. I've gained a lot of insight as a life coach and speaker over the years. I also speak from my own personal experience because I have often been guilty of plenty of the same behaviors you will go on to read about in the coming chapters. Both my personal and professional experience gives me the ability to be transparent with you about the challenges we face as men and offer insight on how to overcome them.

GOD WILL BE THE GUIDE

I take a very practical approach to breaking down issues and providing solutions. However, spirituality is the foundation throughout the book. You may already understand the importance of seeking and following God's guidance in your life. If not, you will see why it's absolutely essential as we go along. This isn't about preaching to you and getting churchy. It's about giving you the ingredients I'm confident you need to generate greater success in your life and in your relationships.

Read along with an open mind and it will make things much easier to receive.

I WILL KEEP IT REAL

I may say some things you agree with. I may say some things that make you want to curse my name, but either way, I promise to keep it real no matter what. You may experience some resistance to what I lay out for you, but know I'm being completely honest about the topic at hand, man to man.

No matter what I say, you still have to make the choice to embrace it or reject it. Just keep this question in mind as you read, "Has my way of doing things been working for me?" I also encourage you to take what is discussed here and pray about it. Don't just decide based on what seems logical to you. Go to God in prayer and verify that what is being said is what you need to accept as truth. This will help guide you in the direction you need to go.

Women have tons of professional resources to help them navigate the waters of relationships. These resources allow them to learn how to overcome the issue(s) keeping them from finding the love they desire. Now, this book will do the same for men who desire the same professional guidance and insight because we too need to know how to accomplish the same results.

I'm confident you're going to find this book and the information it contains very valuable. Some of the information will be familiar to you and some of it may be brand new to you. Take what applies and begin implementing these things in your life as soon as possible.

Be willing to try new things if you haven't been getting the results you desire with your current routine. The definition of insanity is to keep doing the same thing over and over expecting different results. Stop the insanity! I know you're ready for better results in life, and ready to find the woman you can be proud to call your wife. With that said, there is one more point I need to make and discuss before we continue. Especially for any man reading this that is still a bit skeptical about marriage.

MARRIAGE WAS MADE TO BLESS YOU

"Marriage sucks! It all goes downhill once you say, "I do." Women will switch up on you, deny you sex, and constantly look at you like you stole something. It just isn't worth the investment and putting yourself in position for her to take half of your assets. So, here's some advice; don't get married!"

I hope you realize; I don't honestly embrace anything said in the last paragraph. I was merely echoing the voices of the many men who have taken this negative stance on marriage. What these men who claim they are "just trying to help you" fail to realize is that marriage was never the problem. Who they chose to marry was the problem. Not accepting the effort and responsibility needed to make a marriage work was the problem. Being unwilling to properly communicate and address any and all issues was the problem.

The list can go on forever, but the point is that marriage in and of itself is not the problem. Marriage is a beautiful experience when done with the right mindset and with the right person. Marriage was created as a blessing to you, not a hindrance. This is why the scripture says in Proverbs 18:22, *"He, who findeth a wife, finds a GOOD THING."*

It can be better than good; it can be great! However, that doesn't mean everything will be perfect. It also doesn't mean that you can pick any woman you want, and everything will work out just fine. No sir, marriage takes work. Like most things of great value, it also requires great effort.

You may be thinking, "What's the point? Nowadays you can get just as much from dating as you would from marriage. It doesn't make sense to lock yourself into such a serious commitment, when you can technically give less and possibly get more." This is a fair assumption. Times have changed. Men are receiving an abundance of wife benefits without having to put a ring on it, which makes it very tempting to keep things as casual and uncommitted as possible.

Well, I hate to be the one to tell you, but you will pay a price one way or another. By not creating the stability and security marriage can bring (because it is an expression of value to many woman) you will start to create bigger issues in your relationship in the long run. You also leave yourself open to more distractions because let's be real, if we haven't signed the "contract" we will be more willing to entertain other offers.

Not fully committing may seem like a good option, but if the woman is truly meant for you, then you don't want to play games.

Understand that marriage is not your enemy. If the woman you're with is not one you could see yourself marrying, then stop wasting your time and hers by dragging out the relationship. It's a dead end and you know it. Staying in the relationship will only keep you off the path you really need to be on and keep you from getting the woman God truly has for you. If you don't know what that path is, this is where you need to go to God in prayer to find out.

It's important for you to learn to seek God's specific guidance in your life.

At the end of the day marriage is a great thing to embrace. You just have to be mindful of the things needed to help you create success in marriage and the importance of going into it with the right person. I will touch more on these aspects in the upcoming chapters. The fundamental ideas discussed in this section are good first steps to get you on the right track and in the right mindset as you continue to read further.

My prayer as you continue to read this book is that you will learn many of the things needed to start moving in a more positive direction in life and in love.

● ● ● ●

Chapter 1
HE WHO FINDS A WIFE, NOT HE WHO CHASES A WOMAN

> *He who finds a wife finds what is good and receives favor from the LORD.*
> –Proverbs 18:22 NIV

The journey to finding a wife is often long and tiresome. It's all good if you haven't reached this stage in your life yet. You might be more focused on "having fun" and "experiencing life" right now. Maybe you just don't feel ready to take that big of a step and you're still working on getting your life in order. Whatever the reason, it just may not be time for you right now, which is understandable.

However, at some point you will eventually grow tired of running around or rolling solo and reach a place in your life where you desire to experience the consistency, love, and support found in marriage. Trying to go through life on your own can get tough. Having the right woman by your side can have a huge positive impact on your life and your ability to achieve greater things. So now the question becomes, how do you find a wife?

We've been taught to believe that men are supposed to be the hunters and that it's a man's job to go out and find his wife. It's also believed that if a man really wants a woman, nothing will stop him from going after that woman. To all these preconceived notions I say, "Blah, blah, blah!"

Man don't believe the hype or the naysayers. Be careful with feeding into this type of thinking. You might have been taught that it's on you to go after a woman and find a wife.

However, that isn't exactly the case and shouldn't be taken at face value. Don't get me wrong, I'm not against men pursuing women. In most cases however, men are interpreting the act of pursuing or what "finds" means as the scripture instructs us, the wrong way. This inaccurate perception of what it means to "find" tends to work against us. "Finds" begins to look more like "chase."

It's true that if you truly desire something of value, you must be willing to put in the work required to receive it. However, you have to go about it in the right way. With that said, it's important we go about "finding" a wife the right way. In order to do this, we need to get clarity on what "finds" really means and how it differs from chasing in the pursuit of a potential wife.

Let's start by looking at the definitions of *find* and *chase*. Dictionary.com gives us the following definitions.

> **Find** *(v)*: 1.) Discover or perceive by chance or unexpectedly. 2.) Recognize or discover (something) to be present. 3.) A discovery of something value.

> **Chase** *(v.)*: 1.) Pursue in order to catch or catch up with. 2.) Try to contact (someone) in order to get something owed or required. 3.) An act of pursuing someone or something.

Notice *find* means to stumble upon, meaning you weren't or didn't have to be looking for it to find it. When we apply the correct definition to pursuing women, you essentially just need to learn how to recognize when you have come across a woman of great value to you.

Chase involves the act of running after something to catch it. When you are forced to chase someone, it typically means the person is being elusive and is making it a challenge to be caught. Some people like to believe that men want a challenge, that men enjoy the "chase" because they should always be the "hunters." There may be some truth to that perception, but only to a certain extent.

Ask yourself this question? Do you really want a woman who is intentionally being difficult? Do you really want to feel like you're making all of the effort while she sits backs and makes you jump through hoops?

Be honest here. Most likely you don't. When you're truly into her as a person and want a genuine relationship, you want to feel confident that the feelings are mutual. Most men desire a woman of standards, a woman not easily gotten by just any man, but this doesn't mean she should make you chase after her.

Beware of a woman who wants you to take the route of chasing her.

IF A WOMAN MAKES YOU CHASE HER, THERE IS A PROBLEM

Some men don't see chasing after a woman as a problem. However, they aren't looking at this issue correctly. Understand that there are two main reasons why a woman will make you jump through a bunch of extra hoops to win her over:

1. She isn't genuinely interested in you or being in the relationship.

2. She's holding on to fears from the past that have her very guarded and these fears are keeping her from opening up to you fully.

Just because she isn't truly interested doesn't mean she wouldn't get with you when it's all said and done. However, know that if she isn't truly into you, then getting with you would be more about circumstance rather than a genuine connection existing between you two. That right there is a setup for a failed and miserable relationship.

When you look at the love stories told in the Bible, you won't find one example of a man having to "chase" after a woman. The closest example may be the story of Jacob and Rachel. For those of you not familiar with the story, Jacob saw Rachel and knew immediately he wanted to take her as his wife. He went to Rachel's father and agreed to work for him for seven years and then he would be able to marry Rachel.

Well, after the seven-year term was up, the father tricked Jacob into marrying his eldest daughter instead. Jacob then had to work another seven years in order to take Rachel as his wife. Looking at the effort Jacob had to put in to get the woman he wanted, you might want to interpret this as him chasing her.

However, this isn't the case at all. Rachel didn't make Jacob chase her. Rachel's father took advantage of Jacob's desire for his youngest daughter. So, basically the only story of a man somewhat "chasing" a woman in the Bible involves him getting played. Which brings me back to the main point, if a woman makes you chase after her, something is wrong, and you are setting yourself up for bigger issues.

In some cases, she may have genuine feelings for you. Admitting this to herself scares her. She's probably guarded from past issues and uses walls as a defense mechanism to try to maintain control over her feelings and emotions. She will try to claim you need to prove yourself, but no matter what you do, it will be a struggle trying to make progress in the relationship.

If you're "Mr. Perfect" this could actually make things worse. She may view you as too good to be true. This will only heighten her worries and increase her doubts, causing her to purposely look for things to fall apart. This type of behavior is completely out of your control and doesn't mean you aren't putting forth a genuine effort or that she doesn't have genuine feelings for you.

All of this is a result of her not taking the time needed to heal from past hurts. A choice she has to make on her own. You can't force it on her and trying to ignore the need for it will just set you up for larger issues later down the line in your relationship. Issues that could have been avoided altogether.

SHOW DESIRE, NOT DESPERATION

When a man is chasing after a woman, many times he's acting out of desperation. Even if he doesn't realize it, or didn't intend to, this is how it looks from the outside looking in. The more a woman makes you chase her, the more desperate you look. Desperation does not look good on a man. It will cause you to inevitably lose the respect of the woman you're chasing when you act in this manner.

A woman wants to feel valued and desired. So, naturally you may try your hardest to show her that you do in fact desire her and are serious about your position. That is perfectly OKAY, but a line has to be drawn. You're probably wondering where you draw this line and how do you know if you've crossed it or not?

You've crossed the line if:

- Your situation feels one-sided

- Your putting in majority of the effort

- The woman you're pursuing is resisting your advances, and seems bothered by your attempts

- She's filed a restraining order against you

- Her family members are threatening to do you bodily harm if you don't leave her alone

All of the above are clear indications that you have crossed the line and need to rein yourself and your unhealthy desire back in. It's important that you're mindful of not crossing the line between desire and desperation as you pursue women of interest.

The rule of thumb is to remember to *show desire, not desperation*.

Learn to express yourself and your desire in a confident and poised manner. You can only do your part in the progression of a relationship by stating your interest clearly and in a positive way. It's not your place to ram it down her throat, hoping she gives in.

Yes, some men appear to have success with this approach, but things are not always what they seem. This type of overly aggressive approach is more likely to work against you, not for you, in the long run. If you genuinely want a great relationship, don't act desperate. Allow her to reciprocate your interest, which is just as important to the health of the relationship.

THERE HAS TO BE A
MUTUAL EFFORT

A great relationship is about two individual's willingness to work together, support each other, and a mutual desire to take care of each other's needs. With that said when you find yourself chasing after a woman, you have started off on an uneven foundation. Sure, she can eventually catch up and even things out, but if she doesn't, is she really to blame? You have essentially made it acceptable for things to be one-sided, so you shouldn't be surprised if things continue that way.

There is a quote by an unknown author that states "It's not how you start, but how you finish." This is an accurate quote when referring to sports, but in a relationship, how you start sets the stage for how things will continue to go over the course of the relationship. You have to be very mindful of this starting out, so you set the right tone and expectations.

A woman who is genuinely interested and who is not holding on to any deeper issues will have no problem putting forth a mutual effort. She will generally match your intensity. If you slack off, she will do the same, but if you are on top of your game, she will have no problem pouring into the relationship just as much.

A woman's lack of effort is a bright red flag and warning sign of danger up ahead. To ignore the bright red flag is a huge mistake on your part. I'm not telling you to cut her off the minute you notice it, but you do need to address any issues right away. Communicate your concern to her in a positive and loving manner.

Properly addressing the issue will make it much clearer to see if the relationship has any real hope over the long term. If you know you are putting in a good effort and if she isn't doing the same, then you'll know not to continue moving forward with her romantically.

Again, I'm all for men pursuing women and putting in the necessary work to make a relationship happen. However, I don't want you to give in to the mentality of the need to chase. "He who finds a wife," finds a woman who is willing to work with him in building a great relationship, together. If she's being overly difficult and making you jump through unnecessary hoops, then you won't have the necessary foundation for a successful relationship.

Do your part. If she rejects or refuses to accept your efforts, then it's her loss. Getting caught up in chasing after her will become a distraction in your life and will bring you more stress and frustration than it will happiness. Not to mention, you risk the emotional damage it causes, which will have you holding back on the woman that really deserves your attention. You will become the man who can't find his wife, not because she doesn't exist, but because you've become blinded by the disappointment of chasing after a woman you weren't meant to be with.

 **Further Insight:**

1. How do I know when a woman is truly God sent?

   Well, the first step is to go to God and ask Him in prayer. That may be easier said than done because hearing God in prayer isn't cut and dry for everyone. However, prayer is truly where you start from. This is why you have to constantly work on strengthening your relationship with God.

   A strong relationship with God will enable you to hear his voice much more clearly. Many times, we do feel the answer within our spirit, but we try to rationalize it, or convince ourselves that this is just our mind playing tricks on us.

   However, if you go to God in prayer to genuinely seek His guidance, then His voice will always ring loudest. Be still and really tune in as best you can. Aside from going to God, ask yourself if you are truly into the woman as a person or only what she provides. If you truly enjoy her as a person, then you are off to a good start.

2. **What do I do if the woman I love hasn't healed from past issues?**

It's very difficult to deal with a woman when she is still holding on to her past. Every woman handles her lack of healing differently. Know that there will be some level of resistance on her part. However, no matter the level of resistance, you'll need to initiate a calm and loving discussion about it. Don't attack her, talk down to her, or overwhelm her by creating new issues.

Express yourself in an open and honest manner. Offer your support and encouragement and see if the two of you can come to an understanding on how to overcome the obstacles together and move in a better direction. If the situation becomes too difficult and she resists all attempts to work on her problem(s), then unfortunately you have to be prepared to walk away. That doesn't mean things can't work out in the end, it just means that now is not the time.

Let her focus on herself and work on her own issues, while you focus on your growth as a man.

3. What does desire mean to a woman?

A woman's interpretation of your desire will vary. Some women may want a more open expression of your feelings, while others may simply want more of your time. Some women may look for you to communicate with them daily, while others just want you to give them your full attention when you do talk. It can be some of these things, all of these things, or a list of other requirements that translate into the desire they are looking for.

Take time to get to know what speaks to that particular woman's heart. Begin by being willing to take some initiative when it comes to seeing her and communicating with her on a consistent basis. Don't be afraid to express how you feel, just do so in a confident and positive manner. This will help get things moving in the right direction, while you learn more about each other's needs and desires.

● ● ● ●

Chapter 2
YOU'RE FOCUSED ON THE WRONG THING

The successful man,
is the average man, focused.
−Unknown

Dealing with women these days can be difficult. They say they want one thing, but their actions say something entirely different. You try to be the good guy, yet you see so many women reward the bad guys. They claim they can't find a good man, but then turn around and pass one over when another opportunity presents itself. When they do finally embrace a good man, they run the man away with issues stemming from past relationships. It can get downright confusing, but honestly guys, women and their mixed signals are not the real problem.

It's really easy to point the finger and call all women "crazy." However, what does that really solve? You will still find yourself frustrated. You still won't get what you're looking for...a wife. You can have all the men you know join you on a mountain top and scream your disgust with the actions of many women, but it won't do anything but result in a group of women finding a nearby mountain top to scream their disgust right back at you. There is an unfortunate battle of the sexes going on. It's been going on for a long time. Joining in on that battle is pointless. What would be a better use of your time?

Good question. The answer is you have to get to the core of the issue. You've been focusing your energy on the wrong things. You have relinquished your power to see a change because you're too worried about things that are out of your control and that aren't in your best interest to focus on. By making some adjustments to your approach, you'll start seeing a much better outcome to what you desire to achieve...love and a lasting relationship.

CHASE GOD, NOT WOMEN

I mentioned earlier how chasing women is not in your best interest. When you get caught up with chasing women you can easily lose sight of what's important. One of those important things is your relationship with God. He has to be at the forefront of your life, if you truly want to find the woman who is meant for you. No woman can provide you with what God can. Putting so much energy into chasing after women, won't lead you down the best path, especially when you don't give God the time needed to build a proper relationship.

You may have not even realized how much time you've focused on women in comparison to God. Sometimes when you find a woman you love; you can get so caught up in being with her that you don't realize how much it takes away from other areas of your life. You can get so caught up to the point where you essentially put her over God.

Think about that for a second.

Have you ever done things or made certain decisions because of a woman, even though you knew deep inside it wasn't what God would want you to do? Have you ever skipped over your time with God (praying, going to church, etc) because you placed more desire in being with her? Have you ever gotten so consumed with a breakup or relationship drama that it led you to dwell in negativity and ignore how blessed you really are?

If the answer is yes to the previous questions, well then you have experienced placing women over God. Trust me, I understand. It happens to the best of us, and you just have to start being aware of when your focus is shifting too far away from God.

The great thing about correcting this issue is that it will actually get you the results you desire. Whether you realize it or not, a lot of women are attracted to a spiritually grounded man. It helps them feel more secure and it shows a level of discipline that they can admire from a man.

Also, when you focus on God, you start focusing on the things you need to do and areas where you need improvement within yourself. This progression in life will attract not just potential romantic interests, but professional opportunities as well. I'm confident that when you do what you're supposed to do, you'll get what you desire and then some. So, it is to your best advantage to make God your priority.

Chase God and watch the blessings chase you.

DON'T WASTE TIME WITH WOMEN WHO DON'T DESERVE YOU

A previous coaching client I worked with, came to me because he was trying to get his life in order and needed some guidance. He was also trying to recover from a huge heartbreak at the time. The relationship started off great. They were spending time casually and just enjoying each other in the beginning.

She let him know upfront, she didn't want anything serious. At first, he was completely cool with her position. However, they continued to hang out, having a great time, and were consistently intimate. Gradually he started to realize he had deeper feelings and had actually fallen in love with her. Slowly things began to change.

To make a long story short, he wanted more, she wasn't trying to hear it. This created conflict that led to them ending their relationship.

Shortly after the breakup, he meets another woman. She seemed great and they clicked very well. He knew he didn't want to get serious, especially after what he had just gone through. She claimed she was okay with that, but he could tell she was hoping things could eventually turn into more. He knew in his heart he didn't see a future with this woman, but he continued to rationalize why he should continue seeing her and enjoying her company.

His position might make perfect sense to you. This may be a situation that sounds a little familiar because you've experienced it before. Particularly the part where you didn't want the relationship and she did. Maybe you've made the decision to transition from a heartbreaking relationship into a rebound relationship without taking time to heal first. Maybe you've decided to hold on to a woman you knew you didn't see a future with, but who you wanted to enjoy in the present for however long it lasted.

These are all HUGE mistakes for a man to make.

A man of God, who wishes to have a wife one day and create a long lasting and happy relationship will suffer from making these types of mistakes. Whether or not you realize it at the time, you are hindering your path to the blessing of finding the wife you desire. You're wasting your time and hers if you know deep inside, she doesn't make the cut. It isn't an insult to her, it's simply the reality of the situation.

As a man, you'll meet plenty of women you like and find some level of value in. However, many of the women you meet will not have enough value for you to want to take them seriously and view them as a potential wife. You can choose to continue with the relationship, but you run a huge risk of creating unnecessary problems and emotional damage to yourself and her as a result. Especially when you know in your heart she doesn't compare or replace the top spot for the woman you've had the most feelings for.

This may be a tough pill to swallow for you. Many men desire companionship and don't want to pass up a situation that provides any of the benefits we currently desire. However, making concessions in the short run, isn't going to help you over the long term. It will do more harm than good.

The man in the story above finally came to that realization and ended the rebound situation. The woman involved was not happy about it, but it allowed him to remove a distraction that was keeping him from where his focus needed to be at that time, on God and on himself.

You may try to juggle entertaining relationships while you work on yourself, but this is not really beneficial either. The reason it doesn't work is because you don't really notice how much time and energy you give to these relationships when you're in them. This same time and energy could be put to better use. To go without these "stop gap" situations is a necessary sacrifice if you want to increase your chances and your ability to find and receive your wife.

IT'S ALL ABOUT YOU

Remember the finger you were pointing at women and other external factors as the blame for your relationship issues? Well, I want you to turn it around and notice who the finger is pointing to now. The answer is YOU.

The answer to having more success in life and with quality women is YOU. Don't shake your head in disagreement or attempt to dismiss this point. I want you to accept it, embrace it, and live it.

YOU are the key to turning things around in your life, so be open to doing the things that YOU need to do, to get better results.

When we attempt to lay blame on anything other than ourselves, we rob ourselves of the power we possess. I'm not saying outside forces can't hinder you. I'm not saying they don't play a significant role in how things go sometimes. What I am saying is that despite those things, YOU still have the power to do something about them. If you get too caught up worrying about what you can't control, you won't put your energy into things that can help your situation.

For example, when you come across one of these so-called "crazy women," consider the things you do that contribute to the issue. To start, you can improve the process you use and how you select the women you date and are in relationships with. You can do a better job with how you present yourself in order to increase your ability to attract a greater caliber woman.

I'm not trying to make it all your fault. However, it doesn't serve you to point fingers elsewhere and be frustrated with your lack of success. If you know you're truly doing your best, then maybe it just isn't the time yet. God may have other plans for you at the moment. This is why your focus still has to remain on what YOU need to do in your life. You'll achieve so much more this way. Your willingness to always take a look in the mirror first—before placing the blame—will set you up nicely to have a great relationship with your future wife.

Other than choosing "crazy women" to be in relationships with, there is a long list of other reasons men give, as to why they're not having success in their relationships and difficulty finding a wife. Some of these include:

- There aren't enough good women where they live

- Women don't value good men

- Women can't be trusted, they're only after money/status

- Other vague reasons they don't know how to put into words

Have you found yourself saying any of these things as the cause of your lack of success in finding your wife now or in the future?

I want you to know that there are other distractions at work that you might not be paying attention to.

The world is filled with so many things that can grab our focus. If we're not careful these distractions will start to consume us. Some of these distractions can end up serving a greater purpose in our lives, while others can open the door to even bigger problems. Either way, it's important for you to step back and see if where you're placing your energy truly aligns with where it should be.

Are the decisions you're making now wise choices that will produce long term beneficial results? If you desire long term companionship, then make sure the decisions you're making are helping to set you up for long term companionship rather than pulling you further away. Don't look outside yourself to explain your lack of success. Always take a journey inward to get the real answers to your problems. No matter how many external factors might make it more difficult for you, you still have what it takes to overcome these obstacles. It boils down to taking personal accountability for your results now and in the future. It's your responsibility to set yourself up for better. Dismissing your part in the problem, along with a negative mindset towards women will not help you reach your relationship goals. Change your perception, change your approach, and embrace the work you need to put in, to get the results you desire.

 **Further Insight:**

1. Focusing on God, what does that mean to a person who is still trying to understand and embrace a relationship with God?

Start off with the basics. Simply spend more time with God. Make God the main focus in your life and put Him at the center. When you do this, you will start doing things His way. You probably already know this deep inside. An example would be, when you are warned by intuition that your next move is the wrong move and may be hurtful, this is to get you to change course.

However, we often miss the warning or choose to ignore it and proceed only to end up regretting our actions in the end. Learning to choose the right and more positive approach (not to mention less painful) will help push you towards God's way. Taking more time out to pray and read your Bible, to gain more wisdom and understanding, will help you focus more on God and build your relationship with Him.

There are also books you can read to assist you on your journey, because for a lot of men, jumping right into the Bible may be a bit overwhelming and confusing without any guidance. Also, try to find a Bible-based church you can go to and learn from other men, who have been walking with God longer. All of these things will contribute to your being able to focus more on God.

2. **If I'm really into her; how will I be able to determine that she isn't really the right woman for me?**

Praying about it has to be the main part of the equation. You also have to take a step back and allow yourself a moment to properly evaluate the relationship. If you removed the circumstances and the benefits she provides as a romantic partner would you still want to be with her?

Basically, are you truly into who she is as a person, or just what she provides as a woman? If you feel like you don't really know her enough, then you definitely need to start spending more time just talking and seeing if you enjoy her presence.

Also, when it comes to marriage it's all about what you are willing to give, and if you are willing to fulfill your partners needs. So, you should find out what her expectations are, and if you don't feel you can live up to them or that you want to, you should move in a new direction.

3. You say it's all about me, but how am I responsible for the bad choice's women continue to make, by overlooking the good men or doing things to ruin good relationships?

You are not responsible for what women do. However, you have to be careful that you don't internalize their negative behavior to the point where it creates negativity within you. When you do this, you will start to do things that will only make finding a great relationship more difficult for you.

Only focus on what you can control, and that's you. No matter how many women overlook good men, there are plenty that won't. If you are really presenting your best self, and working towards being a better person, it will not go unrecognized. Stay focused on you, and don't allow all of that other stuff to distract or discourage you.

•   •   •   •

Chapter 3
BEING "GOOD" ISN'T "GOOD ENOUGH"

*I am an honest, God-fearing man who
is intensely dedicated to being
the best person I can be...*
–Ricky Williams

Everywhere you look it will seem like the good guys are losing. Especially when you are constantly seeing women "reward" the bad behavior of other men. These so called "bad boys" are usually abusive, disrespectful, and good for nothing. However, they still manage to find a woman, and what often appears to be a nice one at that. I will admit, it can be completely disgusting, and downright frustrating to see this repeatedly, when you have been raised to believe you are supposed to be a "good man."

Why in the world are so many women embracing low quality boys, proclaiming to be men, and then screaming, "I can't find me a good man."

Why are they blatantly overlooking the great guys?

There are plenty of things to take into consideration when trying to understand this issue. However, we're going to focus only on the things within your power to control. Let me start by asking you a question. Is it possible that your good just isn't good enough?

Many men self-proclaim to be "good men," but this might not necessarily be the case. Your family and friends may agree with your sentiment, that you're a "good man," but they don't always get to see the deeper things going on beneath the surface.

Woman you have dealt with in past relationships might have acknowledged, you're a "good man" but they may not always tell you the whole truth. You may indeed be a "good man" by most standards, but are you truly the man God desires you to be? The only way to find out if you're the "good man" you and everyone else think you are is to go to God in prayer, humble yourself, and ask. If you get an answer contrary to popular belief, ask what you need to do to improve.

It's very easy to allow our pride to bli   seeing the many areas in our lives wher change. Even a "good man" still has plent, ᴗ. ιᴏᴏm to be better and gaining a better understanding on how to make that happen is necessary to personal development and growth. So, if you are serious about seeing progress, here are some things you need do.

ACKNOWLEDGE YOUR FLAWS

You can't overcome an obstacle if you're not willing to face that obstacle. In order to face the obstacle, you have to know what you're up against. The first step in growth as a man begins with your willingness to find and accept your weaknesses and flaws. We all have them, so there is nothing to be ashamed of. There is nothing strong or manly about turning a blind eye to them. Ignoring your flaws will simply make you look foolish and you will have to pay a price for them over the course of your life.

Refusing to do an honest self-evaluation, you rob yourself of the opportunity to become a better man. No matter how good you think you are, you are not yet as good as you can or need to be. Could you imagine if Lebron James came into the NBA, simply accepted that he was great, and never practiced or tried to develop his game further? Sure, he would've still experienced some success, but he would have fallen way short of his true potential. For him to achieve a higher greatness, he had to watch film of himself, take constructive criticism, and then work to improve his all-around game.

The process never ends unless your content with achieving less than you truly can.

It may be tough for you to properly evaluate yourself. You will likely need some outside input to help you gain a better and unbiased perspective of yourself. Don't be afraid to go to friends, family, a professional or someone else you can trust for assistance. Ask for their brutally honest opinion of you and the areas you can improve on. Do not take offense to what they have to say, because this isn't about them insulting you. This is about your growth. You need an objective view of yourself, your strengths, as well as your weaknesses, and flaws. This will help you get out of the mindset that you're "good."

You have to do the work but trust me you will see the reward of completing this process in the end.

Don't resist it, and don't be a victim of pride, the all too common mentality that holds men back from their best self.

CHANGING HOW YOU ARE, DOESN'T CHANGE WHO YOU ARE

I come across a lot of men who pridefully state; "I shouldn't have to change for anyone. This is who I am, and people can either take it or leave it."

Well, if you haven't had much success with relationships then clearly, they are leaving it and this approach isn't effective. There is nothing wrong with change. Let me repeat that again, THERE IS NOTHING WRONG WITH CHANGE.

A man who never changes is a man who never evolves into anything greater in life. Change is necessary if you want to continue to see better results in every aspect of your life. Some changes may only require small adjustments, while others will require major adjustments in your thinking, habits, and actions. Big or small, change will need to happen if you desire to get different results than the results you're currently experiencing.

Some men resist change because they may view it as a shot to their manhood. The idea that you need to change, especially to be embraced by a woman, may not feel right to you at the moment. Understand something though, you are not who you think you are. Most likely, you have not even tapped into your true potential as a man yet. So, what changing means here is really about bringing out your TRUE SELF. Some of your behavior and actions in life weren't really true to who you are. They were just products of what you have been through and what you may have been programmed to believe.

It's like a man who was always told he won't accomplish much in life, and then he starts to believe this lie. When you ask him to do better, he responds with "this is just how I am."

NO IT IS NOT! As men of God we are all Kings, but unfortunately you may be walking around with your head down, like you are a mere peasant. It's not that I want you to become full of yourself when I call you a King, but I do want you to recognize that you have untapped greatness inside of you.

Again, your changing isn't about being someone else, it's about truly becoming who you are already created to be.

Don't run from change. Change could be your ticket to the top of the mountain, my friend. You have to stop letting pride and negative thinking blind you from getting to where you truly belong in life and being able to find the wife you desire. The process of your growth as a man doesn't happen overnight, but you don't want to waste any more time. So, start the process as soon as possible.

Your age doesn't indicate where you are in the process or how far you have to go until you reach certain points in your growth and receive your desired blessings.

The length of the process will depend on your character, your maturity, and your willingness to seek God's guidance in your life. I won't lie to you and say this will be an easy or necessarily fun thing to do, but it will undoubtedly be an extremely rewarding process as you continue to press forward and grow more as a man. You will indeed be able to know for sure that you're a "good man" and turn your good into something so great, the right woman, and opportunities will be drawn to you like a magnet.

GOOD GUYS DO FINISH FIRST

We always here the saying, "good guys finish last," but that doesn't always have to be the case. Life is not a sprint, it's a marathon. Good guys may not jump out to an early lead, but if they maintain a good pace and stay focused on finishing, they can easily end up the clear winner. Remember the saying, "it's not how you start, it's how you finish"? Well, this is where it applies perfectly and holds so much truth.

When good guys finish last, it's because they've allowed themselves to take their eye off the prize. When you lose focus, you are more easily discouraged because being a good guy means you won't always receive instant gratification for your efforts. Bad boys may get immediate results with women, but it typically doesn't last, and it lacks true depth and substance.

However good guys who take the right approach can set themselves up for long term sustained success and develop a deep and genuine connection with a woman. Getting caught up in short term benefits is just a distraction and keeps you from seeing the bigger picture. Do you want a few years of fun or a long life of true companionship and love? I know, I know, the "fun" may sound real nice right about now, but it won't give you what you need in the long run.

There are some things you can learn from the behavior of bad boys that will benefit you in your relationships though. It may sound crazy, and you may want to laugh at me, but hear me out. When it comes to women, there are certain characteristics bad boys have, that women are drawn to.

The following list of "bad boy" characteristics are not bad at all; they just get used more often by men who are considered bad boys:

- **Confidence:** Even though for some of these so called "bad boys" their confidence is a mirage. The "I don't care" attitude allows them to exude enough confidence to catch a woman's attention. Good guys aren't always as sure of themselves. They don't always present themselves with the same level of confidence when dealing with a woman they really like, compared to bad boys.

Men who lack confidence make it easier for a woman to intimidate him and this isn't a good position to be in. As a good guy you need to learn how to be confident, without being arrogant. Learn to be humble but still understand and embrace your value. When you present yourself with unwavering confidence it makes a huge impact on how women see you and gives you an irresistible quality.

- **Assertiveness:** Bad boys are always willing to put their foot down. They aren't going to let anybody run all over them, and they have no issue being assertive and standing their ground. A lot of good guys on the other hand tend to be too passive. They are so busy trying to please their woman, and everyone else, that they let people get away with way too much. This causes good guys to be viewed as weak or soft, or as men who can't handle their own.

No woman truly wants a man she can't respect and views as "soft." However, many women will quickly take advantage of a "soft" guy if the opportunity presents itself. To avoid this fate and to get better results in your relationships, you have to learn how to stand your ground.

You shouldn't accept blatant and constant disrespect, and you won't get a badge of honor for taking blow after blow. You simply get damaged. You weaken your position in the relationship or potential relationship. You can be loving and supportive, but you shouldn't accept being a pushover. Practice being more assertive without being controlling.

■ **Be Unpredictable:** What draws a lot of women to the supposed "bad boy" is that he is unpredictable. They can't always call his next move and that keeps them on their toes. It becomes a thrill and provides some excitement in the relationship. Yes, too much of it is unhealthy, but a lot of people eventually get tired of the same old, same old.

Simply incorporate some spontaneity and unpredictability in your routine and it will make a huge difference in your relationship. Don't take on the negative qualities associated with unpredictability, like not calling her for several weeks, or by flirting with another woman in her face. These things are not unpredictable; they're disrespectful and will backfire on you in the long run.

Simple things can make a difference, like taking her to different places and finding new ways to interact and spend time together. Surprising her at work with flowers or to take her to lunch (if this is allowed and you two are at that level) are other good examples.

A willingness to try new things is the key. Throw caution to the wind sometimes, show passion, and don't be too boring. This will increase your ability to have a great relationship.

I am in no way telling you to be a "bad boy," but I do want you to exude some of the traits that they have, that make them more attractive to women. These are good traits to have as a man in general and will produce better results in your love life. Another trait I would add to the above list, but I won't say is that common among "bad boys" is ***knowing how to handle your business***. What does this mean? It means, you have the desire to make something of yourself and have some business of your own.

Women are drawn to ambition and a man's ability to do what he says he is going to do. Don't be fooled by all the losers they entertain, because that is a separate issue that doesn't undermine this point.

Women love a man with a plan and to ignore this fact wouldn't be smart on your part. However, your plan shouldn't evolve around impressing women. It's about you, finding your purpose and passion in life. Discovering the gifts God has placed inside of you that will produce amazing things, once you grab hold of them. Your plan is about you, and what you need to achieve, regardless of what anyone else has to say about it. It just so happens to also come with the benefit of growing you as a man and making you a much more attractive catch for a woman.

So again, I ask you, is your "good" really good enough? Even if you still answer yes, there is still plenty of room for you to grow and become so much better.

Only God knows if it's best for you to reach a new level in life first, before He blesses you with an amazing and loving woman in the form of a wife. He wants to make sure you are truly ready for her and the responsibility that comes along with that blessing. Don't become frustrated and discouraged with how things are right now. Don't continue thinking there are no good women out there and that there aren't any who appreciate a good man.

Just focus on what you need to do to become the man that God created you to be. Trust that in doing this, everything else; including you finding a wife will fall right into place at the right time.

🧠 **Further Insight:**

1. I used to be a "bad boy" and it did seem to work better with getting women. Now that I really want to settle down, they only want to view me as the "bad boy" I used to be, which causes a problem. How can I change that perception?

This is one of the reasons, why being a "bad boy," isn't a good thing in the long run. You may be able to get some immediate results, but you increase the chances of creating a bad image for yourself that's hard to get rid of. If you find yourself in this position, you have to focus on showing the new you on a consistent basis. You can say you have changed all you want, but actions speak louder than words. It's not just the actions you take when you are in front of the woman you want, but the actions you take even when she is not around.

Remember that people are always watching you. This leads to people always talking about you. So, if you think you can slack off when she's not around, don't be mistaken. Word travels fast. You want to increase the chances of the word being spread about your new, good side, by always striving to take a positive approach in life. At some point you will start to be recognized for the man you are today and not the man you once were.

Be patient though, this won't happen overnight.

2. If God is in control, shouldn't being myself be good enough for the woman God has for me?

Yes and no. You definitely want to be yourself, but the question is; are you truly being the best version of yourself? Due to past experiences you may have walls up that are hindering you from really being your true self. You may also still be learning who you are. In that process you have yet to truly define yourself.

Definitely be you, but don't take the, "accept me as I am" approach as a way to validate your lack of effort to work on yourself for the better. You should always be open to constructive criticism and all the ways you can improve. It will only work to your benefit when you do.

3. I am willing to work on myself and be a better man. However, it seems that a lot of women are always finding something to complain about. Is it just a lost cause with some of these women?

To some extent it is a lost cause if a woman is always trying to find something to complain about. She may have a deeper issue that has nothing to do with you, and there is nothing you can do to change that. She has to make a choice to address it, but you have to always make sure that you are not behaving in a way that validates her taking issue with you and what you do.

● ● ● ●

Chapter 4
GOD'S PROCESS IS THE BEST PROGRESS

Trust in the Lord with all your heart and lean not on your own understanding.
–Proverbs 3:5 NIV

When it comes down to it, there are two paths to walk in life. There is God's path, and then there is the world's path. All of our perceptions and decisions will fall in either one of these two categories. Some people stay on the world's path only and reject God's way. Some walk the world's path while they proclaim to be with God, but their destination won't change. Most of us hop back and forth from both paths. Using the one that may seem convenient at that time, or just from a natural conflict that resides within us to go in a different direction than what may be best for us.

For example, we know the bible tells us to not have sex unmarried, but when we see a beautiful woman we desire, many of us will convince ourselves of every reason why we should let it happen. We choose to ignore the "minor detail" of God's instructions of no fornicating. We know we are told we shouldn't lie, but when we are faced with a situation where we may fear backlash from the truth, we will say what is necessary to get our preferred outcome and throw the label of "white lie" on it. As if that actually changes it from still being a lie.

Making a choice between which of the paths to walk on is a never-ending struggle that we all have to face. It is just part of our human nature, but we all have what it takes to do what's best. In order to do so, we have to gain a better understanding of God's path for us. It is one thing to tell someone "do it because God said so," but it can be much more effective when we can breakdown why a decision is truly in their best interest.

Here are a few things that will help bring some clarity and a better grasp of always trying to stay on the path God directs you to walk on.

YOUR LOGIC IS LIMITED, GOD'S KNOWLEDGE IS LIMITLESS

You may have faced some crossroad situations in life where you needed to figure out which path to take. Many times, deciding on the best path doesn't involve doing what's right vs. committing a sin. It simply boils down to doing what makes sense to you vs. going to God and listening to what He tells you to do. It is a matter of faith and obedience. His path may not make any sense to our logical mind, and so we often reject it. We dismiss its validity based on what we see and hear, but that is a mistake.

Let me give a more practical, non-sin-based example to illustrate this point further. A previous client of mine was in a relationship with a great woman he believed wholeheartedly to be his future wife. The relationship was going great until they got into a fight because of his child's mother. His child's mother had continuously been a thorn in his side and was trying to sabotage his current relationship. The fight caused his girlfriend to want to call it quits and it seemed that she had had enough. He was crushed. He tried frantically to get her back, but with no luck.

He decided to dwell in negativity, and this only created more problems in his life. So, naturally he reached a point where he was ready to give up on the relationship as well. He wanted to find another woman (a distraction) to help him cope and move forward. As we worked together and discussed the situation, I explained to him that this was not in his best interest to do. I advised him to go in prayer and ask God for clarity on the relationship and to find out if his ex was truly the woman for him.

He resisted my instructions at first, saying it was pointless. He had given up hope, she wasn't willing to take him back, and he just needed to accept that. I told him to not make decisions based on his own logic. Instead, he needed to see what God had to say about it and allow Him to instruct him on how to proceed.

He finally prayed about everything. He came back to me, stating that although he was struggling to accept God's answer, due to the circumstances, he still felt God was telling him that his ex was in fact the one. Now that he had clarity on the situation outside of his own logic and emotions, he was able to focus on what he needed to do from there. I reminded him not to bring another woman into the situation because it would only make things worse. He agreed, and from there we worked together to get him focused on his growth as a man, and on addressing the issue with his child's mother.

After taking some months to focus solely on growth, healing, and improving the situation with his child's mother; he was given an opportunity to speak to his ex. They were able to work things out because not only was he able to grow during their time apart, but she also took the time to address some things she needed to work on as well. They were able to get back together and are moving forward with getting married.

The point of that story and this section is to drive home the fact that God sees way beyond what we can comprehend in our limited view of things. He does not work within our logic, and we should not use our logic alone when making decisions in life.

God knows what's best for us now and in the future. He knows what the final outcome is even when things look like they're not going to work out in our sight. You might not know what's waiting around the corner when you walk the path, He has laid out for you, but trust Him because he does. He isn't going to tell you to do something only to set you up for failure. It may look bad at first, but if you know God is in it, then the final outcome will be far greater than you can currently imagine.

• IT'S IN HIS TIMING •

Another reason we struggle with walking on God's path is because we are impatient. When we want something, we want it now. Our anxiousness and impatience will cause us to look for the quickest route to get it. However, many times what comes too fast will not last. It isn't always in our best interest to take the path of least resistance. However, this isn't something we always realize right away, many times it's not until later on down the road that it begins to make sense to us.

It's tough to have to sit and wait on something we desire so strongly. However, the waiting isn't the hardest part; the hardest part is not knowing when we will finally get what we want, and this makes the waiting worse. If you knew you had to wait two months for a new job that would pay you more, and this was a guarantee, then it would be a lot easier to be patient and wait for your time to come.

However, when you are waiting for that same job, and there is no timetable, and no guarantee (from a non-spiritual perspective), well then that wait can drive you crazy. During the waiting period you are more likely to stray off your path and take things into your own hands. However, your hands were not made to control the situation if you truly want to experience the best outcome.

Only God knows the most effective time frame for us to receive our blessings. He knows all the things that need to be done along the way. He knows how every experience will shape your life and the lives of others connected to you. As difficult as it may feel to be patient, it is a must. Although you have to wait, the waiting period isn't about sitting back and doing nothing while you, "put it in God's hands." You still have work to do while you wait. To do nothing is like standing on God's path and not moving, expecting to reach your destination by a miracle or God bringing the destination to you.

Faith without works is dead, so trust and believe that you have to do the work, which is how you actually walk God's path. Don't worry about the distance, just focus on your progress, no matter how small. As you continue to move forward in the right direction, you will move closer and closer to what has been waiting on you all along.

Remember you're not really waiting on God, you're waiting on yourself, to do what you need to do (the work), to get the blessings God has for you.

THERE IS A TESTIMONY IN YOUR TRIAL

When it comes to God, He is not only our Father but our teacher. He wants to provide for us, but He also wants us to learn how to use the tools He blessed us with. This is how we access all that He has for us. There is no lesson in just sitting back as He hands us everything we desire. What greater purpose would that serve? It's like spoiling your children. They may be happy, you may enjoy putting a smile on their face(s), but they will never learn the value of anything if they never have to work for it.

You see, there is great wisdom to be gained when we are pushed to our limits. We get an opportunity to see, how, if we remain faithful, we can overcome anything. We get to see God's greatness shine even brighter when we are dwelling in some of our darker moments. We learn what it takes to rise above and defeat the obstacles life throws at us. We become stronger, and our faith grows when we embrace, and endure God's process. It isn't easy, but nothing that makes you stronger is.

If you want muscles, you have to put in some serious hours working out. If you want to be intelligent, you have to undergo some serious hours studying and learning new things. If you want financial success, well be prepared to put in many hours of hard work and sacrifice to get to the top of your game. This is just the way it works, and it is no different with God and receiving the blessings He has for you. The great thing about God is He will still throw us some easy blessings here and there to keep us encouraged, but we shouldn't be surprised by this, because that is what a loving Father does.

Ultimately, our being patient and waiting on God teaches us two very important lessons as we face and overcome our trials. One, we are more willing to praise God no matter what, and two, we have the ability to help others by providing our testimony. Just like the example I gave you about my client, who after much resistance, went to God in prayer, exercised obedience and eventually, after doing what he was told to do, ended up with the woman he truly loved and was meant to be with. Sharing his story was to encourage you if you are in a similar situation, to not give up.

Do not get discouraged and be sure to focus on the right things. If my client wouldn't have endured his process, I would not have a testimony to share with you. Sure, there are others way I could try to encourage you, but when we can hear about or see someone do it for real, it makes a difference in how willing we are to endure our own path.

Do not give up. Do not allow frustration and negativity to get the best of you or get you off course. Do not allow others to bring you down and steer you away from taking the path that is best for you, which is God's path. Do not walk with your head down. Do not dwell in disappointment. Know that you are blessed and again DO NOT GIVE UP.

Make sure you go to God in prayer and seek his specific direction, in your life and in your relationships. If He says walk away, then walk away. If He tells you to express how you feel to the woman you love, well then pick up the phone or prepare to write an email. Whatever God tells you to do, just do it, and trust that accepting His process will bring you success in the end.

Further Insight:

1. Trying to stay on God's path can be a huge challenge. What are some tips you can give to help with achieving this?

Staying on God's path is definitely a challenge. You have to take it one day at a time and try not to look too far ahead. When you try to look for the finish line, you may get discouraged if you don't see one in sight. Not to mention if you think you've reached the end, but then realize there is still ways to go. It's best to just focus on taking it one day at a time. Focus on what you need to do each day.

When you understand your purpose and set goals, you will have something to work towards. At this point it becomes all about progress and sticking to the plan. When small milestones are achieved it strengthens you and encourages you to hold on, so that you can receive the bigger rewards to come.

2. How does someone gain the patience necessary to endure the process?

Patience comes with practice, even though it may not feel like you'll ever perfect it. Your patience improves when you make the choice to take every little opportunity you can find to use it, which can be pretty often. You have to train your mind and spirit to be okay with waiting.

Reminding yourself to focus on what you can control, and let God handle the rest. There may always come moments where you feel like you have lost all patience, and that is when you need to pray and ask for more. Everything will come in its right time, and you will continue to grow as you patiently wait.

3. When do you know if it's a good time to share your testimony?

It's always a good time to share your testimony. Having the courage to discuss what you've been through, and how you've been triumphant, can be exactly what someone else needs to hear to overcome their own obstacles. You may not even know when it will help someone, and that's why it's hard to pinpoint the best time to speak about your experiences. You just have to trust your spirit, and let it flow when you feel a desire to share it with someone.

A common fear you may experience is the concern that people will use your story against you or that they may throw certain parts back in your face in a negative manner. However, when you share your testimony in the name of helping people, when you own your story, and when you follow God's guidance, there isn't anything they can do that can change the power of your testimony.

●　●　●　●

Chapter 5
FOLLOW YOUR SPIRIT, NOT YOUR EYES

> *Follow the way of love and eagerly desire gifts of the Spirit, especially prophecy.*
> —1 Corinthians 14:1 NIV

A friend of mine met this woman he thought was amazing. Now when I say amazing; she looked good, was smart, had a great job, and carried herself very well. He was so excited about meeting her; he immediately started talking about how "she could be the one." He saw no flaw in her and he knew he wanted her all to himself.

They started dating and everything seemed to be going great. However, he began to learn that she wasn't who he thought she was at all. He found out she was playing and using several men, that she didn't have a job, and that her parents were actually taking care of her. The sweet girl he first met was really a pit-bull in disguise. What looked good on the outside didn't match the truth and turned out to be a nightmare. Slowly, this woman began to drive him mad. He tried to find reasons to keep holding on to the relationship, but finally my friend accepted the fact that he needed to walk away.

When this situation happens one too many times it begins to take a toll on you. You start to form a negative perception of women and become bitter as a result. Man, of God or not, I've seen negative energy consume the mind and spirits of too many men, due to failed relationships with no-good women they once thought highly of. However, it doesn't need to be this way, and it shouldn't.

The problem isn't women in general. The problem is how some men go about selecting these women. We can get blinded by things that may make sense to us in the beginning, but that really don't provide the correct foundation for a successful relationship in the long run. So, how do we make better choices? How can we improve our selection process and get better results?

NEVER TRUST
A BIG BUTT AND A SMILE

Okay, I don't mean that literally. It's actually a saying from a popular song in the 90's, entitled "Poison" for those of you that don't know. There are plenty of nice butts and a smile that you can trust, however you shouldn't allow those two attributes to overshadow who the woman is as a person. Sometimes men get too caught up and infatuated with what they see on the outside, and at times allow it to blind them from the true character of the woman. We still place some value on other things like her personality, but more times than not we get distracted by what we see physically, for example:

- She's crazy! - But she's so fine.

- She's messy and irresponsible! - But she's so fine.

- She's a serial killer! – But, did I tell you how fine she is?

Clearly, I'm exaggerating here, but you get my point. Attraction is important, but good looks shouldn't trump a genuine connection, or blind you from seeing the clear red flags that should make you think twice about attaching yourself to a woman. It only gets worse if you have sex with her, and you deem it to be great! Because now you become even more tempted to overlook the things that will come back to bite you in the long run. Proceed with caution and include the next step in your process.

PRAY ABOUT IT

One of the main things I notice about the clients I work with, especially believers, is no matter how much they have accepted God in their lives, they overlook this vital step when dating and in relationships. The vital step is prayer. You may argue that plenty of people pray about potential partners, which is true. However, many people forget to ask God to confirm if the person is truly the person for them.

You can hope and wish all you want. You can ask God to make it work, and to let her be the one. You can pray for her, and you can pray that you two come together. However, why do all of that when if she isn't the person God has for you, it's not going to work out, and you'll just end up wasting your time. No offense to her, it's just the reality you must face as a man.

Everything that glitters isn't gold. You may find plenty of reasons why you want a particular woman, but that doesn't mean she'll be the right fit for you or that she is your wife. If you want to increase your chances of having a great, long lasting relationship, allow God to confirm that you're choosing the right woman in the beginning. He can see things clearly, when we have our minds and hearts wrapped up in all kind of emotions and desires. Our eyes can deceive us, but our spirit was built to lead us.

YOU HAVE TO ENJOY HER WITHOUT SEX

Technically you shouldn't be having sex before your married. However, let's be honest, you will probably continue to be sexually active before you get married. I'm not here to judge you, and I won't act like I'm not guilty in this regard either. Many men struggle big time in this area, as we attempt to find every possible way to rationalize why it's permissible. For the men who have remained on the right track and abstain, keep up the good work because there are plenty of advantages to keeping it in your pants.

When it comes to finding a wife, sex can actually work against you. Sex will cloud your judgment and may cause you to attach yourself to a woman that will only serve as a hindrance in your life. There are plenty of men that know what I'm talking about, and this is not a game. It's a great idea to take sex off the table when you desire a serious relationship. You need time to get to know her, and that trick she does in the bedroom isn't going to help you see things any clearer. This is about creating substance, and sex can completely throw things off.

If you can't enjoy a woman without having sex with her, then you won't stand a chance with having a happy relationship or a happy marriage. Sex can mask a lot of issues, and when the smoke clears (because it eventually does) you will not like what you see. If you can't enjoy a woman's non-sexual presence, then you have a clear indicator that she is not for you, and you are better off walking away.

If you are serious about finding your wife, then it would be wise of you to heed my advice here. I know it isn't easy, to not get caught up in looks, physical attraction, and our own logic, but don't make the mistake that many other men have made.

It may feel good at that moment, but there is a hefty price to pay for this ineffective approach.

I said it earlier and I will say it again, "your eyes can deceive you, but your spirit was built to lead you." The more you practice listening to your spirit, the more you will understand it and be able to let it guide you. Life is filled with distractions. Some distractions are obvious, but many are so subtle that you never even realize what's happening until it's too late. Be smart and avoid the distractions that may stand in the way of you finding your wife.

Further Insight:

1. I like what I like. Am I really supposed to overlook physical attraction? How am I supposed to avoid getting wrapped in looks?

I am in no way saying that you should overlook physical attraction. I believe that physical attraction is an important component in every great relationship.

However, with that said, looks shouldn't trump the need for a genuine connection with a woman. If she looks amazing, but you aren't truly into who she is as a person, then it won't amount to much in the long run.

Also, be mindful that there is attraction and then there are preferences. You may like and prefer women with certain attributes, but that doesn't mean you may not find yourself attracted to a woman that doesn't typically fit your preferences. As long as there is a genuine attraction as well as a genuine connection, then that should be enough to move forward.

2. You say pray about it, but I thought as men we get to choose our wife? Shouldn't I be able to just pick who I want and make it work?

You can always decide to pick who you want, but that won't make her who you were meant to be with or who you truly need. When you understand that God knows best, then wouldn't it be smart to get His input and guidance on the woman you marry? Plenty of men have gone after and gotten that woman they wanted, only to be miserable later on. It is so easy to get caught up in what we see on the surface, and mistake infatuation with love based on the woman that caught our eye.

Praying and asking for confirmation on your choice is like a safety net to help you avoid falling into a trap. Prayer will allow you to go deeper and gain clarity on the person you're dealing with, and help you have a better idea of who you should or shouldn't be dealing with romantically.

3. Sex is such an important part of a relationship, is it really smart for a man to put that to the side? What happens if you end up with someone, you're not sexually compatible with?

I think taking sex off the table is a very smart move for the man who genuinely wants to find his wife. Sex has the power to cloud a person's judgment, and it has led to a lot of men attaching themselves to women who they weren't meant to be with. Sex can cause you to overlook many issues that will only come back to haunt you later. In order to make better decisions, I think leaving sex off the table is a very good move.

There are a lot of misconceptions about sex and sexual compatibility. Most men view sex before marriage as a must, using the analogy of test driving a car before you purchase. I understand the logic but ask the many married men who are dealing with a lack of sex in their marriage how that approach worked out for them. Trying it out beforehand ensures you of nothing later, because there is more to marriage than that.

Great sex in a marriage with most (if not all) women has a lot to do with the connection you have with her. You can marry a "freak" so to speak, but if you don't know how to pour into her and satisfy her needs, then that "freak" will disappear on you. I get more into this topic in my book "How To Get A Married Woman To Have Sex With You...If You're Her Husband" so you can read more in depth about it there.

Ultimately, it isn't so much about test driving the car, as it is about inspecting the car and looking under the hood.

Get to know her, connect with her, get to know who she is and try to understand her, and from there you will be well equipped to create a great sex life in marriage.

●   ●   ●   ●

Chapter 6
NOT HEALING = MORE HURTING

> *Therefore, confess your sins to each other and pray for each other so that you may be healed. The prayer of a righteous man is powerful and effective.*
> –James 5:16 NIV

No one lives a perfect, carefree life. Everyone goes through trials, and these life experiences often include hurt and disappointment. Some people may not have it as hard as others, but that doesn't change the fact that they still get hit by the ups and downs of life. Always keep in mind the fact that you never know what someone else is going through, just like they often don't know what you're going through at any particular time in your life.

The reality is we have all learned how to wear masks. These masks are meant to conceal so that others have no idea about our pasts and what we may be going through currently. People can't see your past unless you reveal it to them, and because they don't know your pain, they may struggle to understand your path. These experiences and trials shape who you become. How you approach the trials and how you handle them will determine if the impact on your life is positive or negative.

As a rule, men are taught to "be strong" and to "be tough."

We interpret being strong and tough to mean, never crying, sucking things up when times get tough, and dismissing our feelings altogether. We become programmed to ignore our deeper issues, and many of us don't learn how to properly address our issues as a result. None of this behavior is true strength; instead it's a destructive pattern of behavior that will lead to larger issues in your life.

A lack of healing is a major problem with men, and whether you realize it or not, it's causing a lot of damage in your life right now. When you don't properly heal, you hinder your ability to experience great things because you are not operating at your optimal level. When you haven't healed from old wounds you become guarded and can become distant when people try to connect with you.

You may struggle to communicate effectively because you never learned how to. You may have never learned how to express your true feelings. Of course, there is also your concern with how people will receive you in these vulnerable moments, and this only makes you more prone to shut down without trying. The same walls you use to protect yourself are the same walls that are blocking your blessings.

Now that we've identified this major obstacle standing in your way and holding you back from experiencing the healing you need; the question now becomes; how do you overcome this mentality? How can you free yourself from this negative mindset that you've held on to for so long, and that has secretly caused you more problems than you realize? The specific steps you need to take will vary depending on your specific situation.

However, there are some core steps you can begin to take to help move you in the right direction and toward healing.

IDENTIFY THE HURT

Your first step is figuring out what you need to heal from. What has happened to you in your past that you still hold negative feelings towards? Who hurt you? These are the things you want to start figuring out and taking note of. However, being able to uncover unresolved pain can be difficult to do alone. This is why you should highly consider getting professional assistance to help facilitate this process. You also have to be willing to be honest about the things you have been through that have had any sort of impact on you. If not, you will not be able to resolve your issues, and healing will not be accomplished.

GET IT OFF YOUR CHEST

The more you hold your feelings inside, the more likely you're going to explode at some point. All of that pent-up emotion is unhealthy. It can take a toll on both your mental and physical health, and it can stunt your spiritual growth as well. I understand that you may not like being vulnerable and having to open up and let things out, but there is no doubt, it needs to happen. Being unable to express your feelings will kill you slowly, and you don't want that to happen.

Also, understand that if you can't talk about the things that have been weighing down on you, then how can you ever properly address them? Guess what, you can't! Even if you struggle to verbally express yourself or aren't comfortable talking to others about how you feel, another good method to consider is writing it all down.

Writing out your feelings allows you to have an opportunity to get everything out all at once. The act of writing is a pure release and will help take some of the weight off your shoulders. That doesn't mean you should stop there. You might still be interacting with people who have hurt you, and if so, it is in your best interest to let them know how you feel.

Believe it or not, they may have no clue on how their actions have impacted you. By taking a positive and calm approach and being honest with them about your feelings, you will create an opportunity for resolution and free yourself from that negative, toxic energy. I know it's easier said than done but continuing as you are isn't going to help either.

Talking about your issues and feelings in a calm and positive manner to those who have hurt you is a big step to take. Again, you may need to seek outside assistance from a professional, like talking to a life coach such as myself, and working together to come up with a plan of action on moving forward. Don't be afraid to reach out to people who can help you professionally. You can get that monkey off your back for good and start moving in a better direction in life.

You have what it takes to see this through. Now is the time to act. Don't let pride or false feelings of weakness stand in your way of getting the help you need and keep you from healing.

ACKNOWLEDGING THAT YOU'RE HURTING DOESN'T MAKE YOU WEAK

One of the main reasons you may still be holding on to past pain and disappointments, is your pride. Pride can become your worst enemy. I mentioned earlier that many men were taught to be tough and to never show their emotions because it was viewed as weakness. So, you may view expressing your feelings as being weak or soft. You may struggle to take the necessary steps to confront an issue because your pride keeps you from allowing people to see that something is bothering you.

You can get so caught up trying to portray an image of toughness, that you inflict further damage on yourself and the people around you.

Pride is not your friend because it keeps you from learning how to humble yourself. Being humble doesn't mean you have to walk around with your head down, it doesn't make you less of a man, and it doesn't mean you will be taken advantage of. Being humble simply means you allow yourself to embrace correction in life. It means that you never think so highly of yourself that it makes you blind to your flaws and the things you need to improve on. You can't concern yourself with how others perceive you when taking this approach; you do it because it is what God wants from you.

Your ability to turn away from pride will bust the door wide open for growth and healing, allowing you to take the necessary steps toward healing without feeling embarrassed or weak. We all have our weaknesses and our weak moments. It's natural to all human beings. There is strength and freedom in accepting that. It's time for you to make the choice to do what is best for you and put all pride to the side as well as the opinions of others.

FORGIVE, FORGIVE, & FORGIVE SOME MORE

There is no freedom without forgiveness. There is no peace without forgiveness. There is only lingering negativity, further damage, and hindered progress when we as men do not embrace forgiveness. You may have experienced a lot of hurt and disappointment in your life from family, past relationships, or just life in general. Some of these experiences may have cut so deep that the idea of forgiving the individual(s) may seem impossible to you. No matter how hard it seems, or how much you feel they don't deserve it, it needs to be done.

Forgiveness is not for them, it's for you. Holding on to what happened only continues to hurt you, while the other person will live their life according to their path and not look back. You gain no victory and there are no benefits from lack of forgiveness. The rewards only come when you finally release the negative energy from your system by forgiving. Doing so will start to open up the floodgates to positive energy and positive results in your life as a whole and in your relationships. You will be able to allow yourself to truly love and be loved by bringing your walls down. You will free yourself of the very things that have been holding you back. The benefits of forgiveness are well within your reach, all you have to do is make the choice to forgive.

Now you could utter the words "I forgive them" but still continue to feel negatively about the situation. Forgiveness isn't going to be an overnight thing. Forgiveness is an ongoing process. You may have to work at it constantly by fighting back the negative emotions and thoughts that rise up from time to time.

When those moments arise remember these few things:

- Remind yourself that what is done is done, and your focus now needs to be on moving forward in a positive direction.

- Remind yourself to not internalize what others have done to you. Hurt people will hurt people, and their actions were a continuation of the hurt cycle. Don't continue the cycle by holding on to the pain; instead release it from your spirit.

- Remind yourself that you are blessed. Blessed to be alive and blessed to have an opportunity to make so much more out of your life. Do not dwell in negativity, instead focus on the positive and the greater potential your life holds.

Remember that forgiving others is just one side of this story. You have to also forgive yourself. Many times, we hold the mistakes we've made over our own head. Doing this paralyzes you and doesn't allow you to move forward in a productive manner. You have to understand that we all make mistakes. People who succeed have also experienced failure, often many times. The key is to learn from your mistakes rather than dwell on them. Use your mistakes as tools to learn from.

A healthy dose of God's guidance combined with the wisdom from lessons learned will set you up to make much better decisions in every area of your life going forward. If you truly want to be able to find, attract, and keep an amazing woman in a lifelong relationship, you have to do some work within yourself first. The need for healing is so essential to your progress and everyday living that each day you continue to ignore it is another day you're holding yourself back from finding your true path and your wife.

Your strength as a man comes from being able to grow and evolve. As you grow and evolve, you learn how to live life more efficiently and you get the most out of life. Let go of the idea that you have to ignore your feelings and just be tough all the time. That won't get you very far, or at least not as far as you could go if you healed from your past hurt. It's time for a change. You need a new outlook on life and what you can achieve. You will be a better man for walking this path.

🧠 **Further Insight:**

1. After getting things off my chest how will I know that I am ready to take the next step?

As long as you've fully expressed yourself and feel there is nothing else you could add to it, then you are ready to proceed. Many times, people feel a weight lifted off their shoulders immediately when they take the time to get everything out.

Just remember that the goal is to release the tension, anger, pain and hurt from your system, not to simply lash out at anyone. You want to take a positive approach to getting it off your chest. If you use your feelings as an excuse to attack someone, you'll only create more issues that you'll have to deal with.

2. Acknowledging I hurt is very uncomfortable for me. How do I overcome this and not let the fear of how people will judge me, stop me from being able to talk about it?

Unfortunately, no matter what we do in life we will be judged by others. They will choose to view us how they wish, and we should only focus on doing what is truly best for us at the end of the day. Keep in mind that concerning yourself with their views of you isn't going to help you make any progress. Bill Cosby once said, "I don't know the key to success, but the key to failure is trying to please everybody."

Focus on pleasing God and do what you need to do so that you can heal and move forward.

3. What if I'm not comfortable speaking to a counselor. What other options do I have with getting help?

Many people have placed a negative stigma on seeking professional counseling or a life coach. The reality is we all need help sometimes, and it's good to get an outside, unbiased, and professional opinion on the issues you are facing. There is nothing wrong with seeking help from a professional if they can help you achieve your goals. If you wanted to get stronger, would you be against seeking the services of a personal trainer? You probably wouldn't, and I believe you should have this same mindset when considering professional help with emotional and psychological issues that are holding you back from living your best life. If that still doesn't work for you, then be open to reading books that pertain to the situations you're dealing with.

There are also tons of resources online that you can use for personal development, to learn and gain useful insight. Talking to family and friends you feel you can trust will also be a step in the right direction as well, but doesn't replace an outside, unbiased, and more informed opinion. The important thing is to begin getting the help you need. The sooner you do, the sooner you can start experiencing better results.

●   ●   ●   ●

Chapter 7
MEN HAVE TO SUBMIT TOO

*In all your ways submit to him and
he will make your paths straight.*
–Proverbs 3:6 NIV

Men have been taught that the man is supposed to be the head of the household, and so we have adopted this way of thinking to some extent. Are you ready to stick out your chest and demand your respect? We're told the man is supposed to lead, and the woman should be willing to follow or submit. Most men don't have a problem accepting the thought of a woman acting in this manner.

However, leading has nothing to do with bossing your woman around. The reality is, if you want a woman to follow you, you have to be able to lead her. You might have bought into the idea of equality in relationships which is a great thing, but this doesn't mean you should ignore your **ability** to lead as a man.

Another issue in relationships today is the fact that a lot of women aren't embracing submission anymore. The rise of the independent woman has thrown things off significantly. Some women are trying very hard to get men to submit to them. It's getting crazy, and more and more independent women claim they don't need a man. When you try to talk to them about submission, it's like you just uttered fighting words. They aren't having it, and this creates huge problems in relationships because it throws off the natural order of things.

Not all women are like this, however. There are plenty of women who have no problem embracing submission. They understand the biblical principle of submission and are willing and ready to accept it. Believe it or not, even some of the same, "I don't need a man," independent women are secretly okay with the idea of submission in their relationship.

I know that sounds off, but understand something, their issue isn't really about submitting, it's about putting their trust in a man and fearing that he will let them down. They have been hurt too many times in the past, or have witnessed other women get burned, so they avoid it at all costs. They fear being vulnerable, and in many cases, there is nothing you can do about it. They have to heal from their past issues as well, and it's their responsibility to work on them. However, you still have to ask yourself something.

Are you truly presenting yourself as a man worthy of leading in your relationship and as someone who is worthy of being submitted to?

Now let's get something straight, leading is not about being a dictator. You don't get to bark out orders, and ignore your woman's feelings, if you truly want the relationship to be successful. Leading is not about her obeying you or doing as you say, or never questioning you about your actions. Let's take a quick look at the definition of lead:

> **Leading** means guidance or leadership, especially in a spiritual context.

> **Leadership** is defined as an act or instance of leading; guidance; direction.

As you can see leading is about guiding and providing direction. However, if you don't know where you need to go or how you need to do things, then how can you properly lead anyone else? More importantly, you lead by example. You have to be open to learning, growing, and practicing different approaches in order to find the best one to enable you to move yourself and your relationship in the right direction. Don't let pride or negativity blind you or keep you from accepting your responsibility to lead in your relationship.

Many men haven't been provided with the proper examples of how to lead, so we often don't have a clue of what a submission worthy man looks like. You may have a vague idea, or your own perception of what this looks like, but that doesn't mean it's correct. You may think that being a provider and protector qualifies you as a man worthy of a woman's submission. I would agree that this plays a part in the bigger picture, but it goes much deeper than that. It's not enough to provide and protect, if you truly want to position yourself to be a man worthy of submission, there are some deeper principles to consider.

YOU CAN'T LEAD WHEN YOU DON'T KNOW HOW TO BE LED

A leader leads, but also knows how to follow. If you're not open to being taught, you will struggle with learning how to teach others effectively. If you never learn how to be led, then you will struggle with leading effectively. This is simply how it works. First, you have to be willing to humble yourself. It's that humble spirit that will allow you to grow. It will equip you with the tools to make others feel more comfortable accepting your guidance and direction. You can be confident and humble, but when you crossover into arrogance you undermine your chances of seeing positive results and won't be an effective leader.

Getting caught up in arrogance and pride is the downfall of many men. It makes you act foolishly, and you will not be able to see the error in your ways. The energy you give off will be toxic and result in your pushing your woman away or making her resistant to fully submitting to you. I know what you're thinking. A lot of women give in to that type of man all the time. Understand that this is being done for reasons that are not healthy, and at some point, both parties will pay a price for it. If you want a happy and healthy relationship, don't get caught up in the bad behavior some women put up with and view as acceptable.

When you learn how to be led by God, and how to accept God's leadership in your life, this will help you become a better leader. God leads by example. God is patient, kind, trustworthy, wise, loving and caring. These are the same qualities you should develop to help you lead in your relationship. If a person was talking down to you, and devaluing you and your opinions, you would most likely reject their guidance. This is the very thing you don't want to do to your partner. A process of growth will occur when you allow God to lead you, and you will be better equipped to lead in your relationship.

RESPECT IS GAINED, WHEN RESPECT IS GIVEN

When you know a person doesn't consider your input, talks down to you, and devalues you, you would probably reject their guidance. If this is your style of leadership then you can expect your partner to reject your guidance and not follow you as well. I think it's very important for you to truly process this point.

Many times, we forget that we have to give what we want to receive in return. What you put out there is what you will get in return. To think that you can speak to someone any-kind-of-way and expect positive results is very wrong and misguided.

You can demand respect all you want, but the question is: are you respecting others? Even if you feel that a person in a specific situation doesn't deserve it, as a man you have to set the example, and their opinion or behavior should not cause you to stoop to their level. You are better off walking away. Because once you start down the path of disrespect, you open yourself up to be disrespected in return. Even in disagreements, you can still remain respectful in your opposition. Losing your composure isn't a sign of strength, it's actually a sign of weakness, and it's something every man needs to be aware of.

I'm making a case for respect in general here, but let's remember this is also about finding your wife and your desire for her to submit to you in your relationship. The more she feels valued and respected in the relationship, the more she will be willing to submit. If you're with a woman who despite your respectful approach is disrespectful towards you, she needs to go.

Respect is a two-way street; give it and you should receive the same in return. However, you have to respect yourself first and a disrespectful woman doesn't respect herself, so she won't respect you as a result. If you allow yourself to be run over by blatant negativity and disrespect on her part, then you're not respecting yourself either. You can dress it up by saying your being loving and patient, but you simply look weak and foolish. You will never be able to earn her respect.

The cure is not to retaliate or become aggressive in a negative way. You simply have to show that you won't stand for it by walking away, and not accepting that kind of treatment. You will have to love and let go, and only entertain relationships where there is mutual love and respect.

IF GOD ISN'T LEADING, YOU'RE WALKING IN THE WRONG DIRECTION

As a man of God, you are likely (at least you should be) looking to be in a relationship with a woman of God. If this is indeed the case, then she will be looking to see a good spiritual foundation in your life before entertaining a relationship with you. She will look to see if you go praise God, pray, and how you live your life as whole. All these things will be examined as she decides whether to embrace you and the possibility of a future with you. This is a good start on her part, but it isn't exactly enough for her to make a proper decision, and the same should go for you as well.

She may look good on the surface, and seem to be living a God centered life, and for most men this will be enough for them to move forward. However, it isn't enough of a solid foundation for starting a relationship. A willingness to go to God and follow his direction at the first sign of real interest will give you both the clarity on whether you should proceed with a relationship. If you do all the religious stuff, but operate daily within your own logic, then you will still experience trouble in your relationships. It will end up being a dead-end situation.

It's like riding in God's car, but still wanting to use your own GPS. You may think you're going the right way but will soon find out you're going in the wrong direction.

When a woman feels confident that you are truly trying to walk with God, then it makes it a lot easier for her to walk with you. She can trust your leadership more because she knows it isn't about your own selfish desires or limited opinions. Her trust will be in your trust in God's direction, and she will have confidence that you're doing what is in the best interest of both your lives, when she chooses to walk with you. When you let God lead you, you will be amazed at the difference this makes in the success of your relationships.

Everyone has a position to play. You, the team captain and God being the head coach creates the proper structure for a long-lasting relationship and potential marriage. She is no less valuable then you are, because without her, there is no team. You both have to work toward strengthening your relationship with God individually and collectively in the relationship. You should be pouring into her the love and respect she deserves. Consider how she feels. Make sure she feels like a valued team member and keep up the moral by putting God first in your relationship and letting Him call the shots. All of this will help make you the man worthy of her love and her submission.

Further Insight:

1. I can understand your points about submission and taking correction. However, will doing this shift the balance of power and respect in the relationship?

Not at all. Remember your submission is to God first, and when you follow His guidance you will get the best results in your romantic relationships and life in general. It isn't about who has the most power in the relationship. It's about both of you working together to create a loving, supportive, and fruitful union. If you make the submission about becoming a "yes man," then that can lead to other issues that you don't want to create in the first place. However, that doesn't mean that you shouldn't allow her to take the lead in the areas she's stronger in. This doesn't mean you should place all the burden on her, or become a doormat in the relationship, learn to maintain a proper balance.

2. How should I handle things when I am doing
   what I'm supposed to do as a man, and yet
   the woman refuses to accept my leadership,
   and give me my respect?

   If you are treating your woman like your
   queen, and she refuses to respect you as her
   king, then you simply have to remove her from
   your kingdom. Make sure you talk to her about
   the issue first before you overreact. Make sure
   there isn't something you're doing that may be
   contributing to the issue. If you properly
   address things in a positive and loving manner,
   and she still shows disrespect, then proceed
   with your decision to let her go. If you
   continue to accept her disrespectful behavior,
   she will continue treating you that way
   because you've given her permission to behave
   this way. At that point you will have nobody
   to blame but yourself.

3. If a woman wants to take the lead, I say let her. I'm not going to go back and forth with her about it. What's wrong with embracing the equality they say they want and allowing her to handle most things in the relationship?

The problem with this approach is that in most cases it will eventually become a problem. A lot of women have a very independent mindset not because they want to have one, but because they've felt they had no choice in order to protect themselves. So when they get into a relationship, they may struggle with letting that independence go. If you play into that struggle by handing everything over to her to handle, you will pay a lofty price for it and it will be used against you when it's all said and done. It will get to a point where she is frustrated with you for not taking more initiative and playing a bigger role in lessening her burdens.

Even though this is a problem she helped create, you need to focus on solving it, not adding to it. Talk to her about her resistance in allowing you to express your love for her by trying to do things for her. Set the standard of how things should go, consider her feelings, and work with her to solve the issues. You two are equal partners, but that doesn't mean you shouldn't still show a willingness to lead and be there for her in the way that will truly speak to her heart.

●   ●   ●   ●

CONCLUSION

A lot of men today don't talk to each other enough. Many may talk sports, hobbies, and women; however, we don't have enough of the deep discussions that help us grow and evolve as men. Too many of us tend to look the other way when we see our family, friends, and acquaintances behaving in ways that aren't healthy. The reason why; no one ever tried to help us, or it could be we just don't feel comfortable taking that position because it is unfamiliar. It's easier to say "that's none of my business" rather than step in and try to direct another man to a better path. Some men may say something, but this needs to happen more often.

We need to work together to change this behavior. We need to share positive wisdom with each other and uplift each other. We need to hold ourselves and others to a higher standard and start establishing a better, more effective approach to manhood, communication, and our relationships. When we see other men abandon their children, we need to call them out on it.

When we see men being abusive and unloving, we need to get them some help. When we see men ready to fight over nonsense that serves them no purpose, we need to encourage them to take a more peaceful route to resolving their issues. It's time that we start helping each other and in order to help someone else we have to be willing to help ourselves. We lead by example.

The core of this book is about giving you the tools needed to work on being a better man. By doing this you begin to tap into the power you have to create better results in your life and in your relationships.

God is at the forefront of everything I've discussed. When you truly accept and begin to implement the principles covered throughout this book, you will set yourself up for greater things in your life and be equipped to make a positive impact on the lives of other men as well. You'll be able to act as an example. You'll be a man other men can respect and look up to.

When you follow the instructions given here and take the time out to work on your inner self, the result will be greater success in life and the blessing of finding a wife. The process becomes so much easier when you learn to focus on God first and then you in that order. Life shouldn't be just about finding any good woman to marry, but about finding the woman God has created especially for you who will help you on your life's journey. I'm confident in your ability to find her if you take the time to do the work required. Never stop learning, never stop growing.

●   ●   ●   ●

POINTS TO REMEMBER

1. **Show Desire Not Desperation.** Desperation reeks of fear and uncertainty. Acting out of desperation is not attractive or to your advantage. Remain confident and express your desire in a positive and effective manner.

2. **Chase God Not Women.** Chasing after women is a huge distraction and steers you off your intended path. Don't allow women to come before God and you will be able to receive the blessings and the woman that is truly meant for you.

3. **Good Guys Can Finish First.** Don't believe the hype about women not wanting a good guy. They desire a well-rounded man just as men desire a well-rounded woman. Be open to improving aspects about yourself that will make

you the good guy almost any good woman would be happy to have.

4. **God Is Not Limited By Our Logic.** Proverbs 3:5 says it best, "Trust in the Lord with all thine heart; and lean not unto thine own understanding." Your logic can only take you so far, while God can take you wherever He wants you to go. It won't always make sense to you, but God always knows best. Trust Him.

5. **What Looks Good Isn't Always Good For You.** This doesn't mean you should ignore the importance of physical attraction. It means you shouldn't allow yourself to be blinded by her shell. Pay attention to the more essential things, like her ability to be supportive, open up to you, loving, and just providing a source of positive energy in your life; that way you can notice any red flags in advance of getting too involved. Also remember, just because she is a good person, doesn't mean she is the right person for you. Be willing to get God's input before moving forward in the relationship.

6. You Need To Heal. Don't go another day running from your issues. Acknowledge them and face them, and if you don't know how, be open to seeking professional assistance with figuring it out. The longer you hold onto negativity from the past, the more you will experience negative results in your life and in your relationships. Now is the time to change that, for good.

7. Be Willing To Submit. At the end of the day God knows better than we do. Trust in Him and always seek His guidance first concerning matters of the heart and in all of your relationships. Submission is not just a principle for women; it's also for men as well. Remember to lead by example. Your submission to God will give her an example to follow and make her more accepting of the order of the relationship.

●　●　●　●

MORE Q&A

1. How do I begin the process of working on me before a relationship, and is there an age that I should be looking to start by?

You simply start by shifting your focus, taking a deeper look within, and making time to talk to God in prayer. There isn't a particular age you should start the process. The best time is always now! The sooner you get started the better. Great things are waiting for you, so there is no reason to postpone the process.

You may feel very comfortable where you are, but are you truly happy? Do you truly feel you are where you belong? Are you genuinely okay with how things have been going, or do you want better results? The answers to those questions will make it clearer if a new approach is needed.

2. How specific should I be in prayer?

Be as specific as you can be. Pray to God like you would express yourself to a best friend. Remember that God sticks to us closer than a brother and you can trust in Him fully to lead you in the right direction. He is also your Father, and therefore loves you like no one can. So just talk to Him openly in whatever way you feel most comfortable. He knows how you're truly feeling so there is no sense in holding back. You may think that if He knows, then why the need to be so specific in prayer?

Well, it goes back to you practicing expressing yourself. The more you do it, the better you get at it. Plus, it's also a good release for you, leaving no room for tension or anxiety.

Also, praying helps bring underlying issues to the forefront that are important and that may need to be addressed. Learning how to articulate yourself and being specific about what your wants and needs are is essential in learning how to communicate effectively in any relationship. Who better to practice with then God?

3. Do I really have to take sex off the table? I
   mean that is a really tough pill to swallow,
   especially when you are used to being
   sexually active in relationships.

To be honest, you don't have to do anything
you don't want to do. The choice is yours.
However, know that by not doing so you can
hinder your growth as a man and your ability
to better evaluate the women you have
interest in. Sex may feel great at the time, but
it is a huge distraction in relationships. You
may start to give sex too much attention and
this takes your focus away from what you
should be concerning yourself with.

As I mentioned before, sex will cloud your
judgment. You will often attempt to rationalize
why you should continue having sex, but deep
down you know better. Attempting to stop
having sex cold turkey is very tough for some
men, but if you stick with it, make the
decision, and stay focused you can make it
happen. Try going without sex for three
months to start. If that number just gave you

an instant headache, shorten it to a period of time you feel comfortable with.

During this time create a few goals for yourself that you can accomplish and focus on. Things that you might have wanted to do but haven't done in the past. See for yourself how much more efficient you become and how much more you get done. Also, use the time as an opportunity to get to really know the woman you're dating or in a relationship with.

You'll be able to see for yourself how much more you're able to learn about her and be able to determine if she is really a woman you should entertain long term. I'm confident you will notice a difference in the relationship and the connection you foster as a result, and you may become more willing to embrace this method going forward.

4. I feel that I have lost myself in the pursuit of looking for a wife. How do I avoid falling into that cycle again as I try to get myself together?

This is why I discourage men from chasing after women. It's very common to lose yourself because you become so consumed with getting her that you lose sight of everything else.

Again, too much attention placed on the chase causes other more important aspects of your life to take a back seat. You suffer even more in the long run, especially when the chase doesn't produce the results you wanted. To avoid this cycle, you have to first build yourself up and know your value.

When you know you are truly a great man, not just a good one, but a great one, you will be less likely to behave this way. You can stand strong and be more confident in your approach. You will show your desire and willingness to put in the work to build a relationship, but you will be less likely to slide into desperation mode trying to prove your worth to her.

Let your worth shine through your everyday living as a man. If she can't see it, then maybe she's blinded by her own issues, and those are hers to deal with. Or maybe she simply isn't the one to see it, because there is better woman waiting for you just around the corner.

So, as I have stated many times throughout the book, focus on your growth as man. Don't try to force yourself on any woman.

Give it to God and trust Him with the process. This will help you avoid falling back into unhealthy past patterns of behavior and will help you learn new and better ways of attracting interested women to you.

5. Define the role of a good man and a good woman?

Rather than define what a good man or good woman is, I will define the role of a great spouse. The role of a great spouse is to love and support their partner. You have to be willing to pour into them in a way that truly speaks to their heart. To act with honesty and openness, to have a positive approach to communication, and the willingness to resolve any concerns or issues that may surface in the relationship.

To submit to God and walk together on a path that is in the best interest of the union. When you are willing to take on that role, everything else can and will fall into place.

A relationship and marriage aren't about what you can get, but rather what you are willing to give. Wait for the woman you are meant to be with. The woman God has approved. The actual woman meant to receive all that you have to give. This way you know your efforts won't be in vain.

Keep God first. Let God be the only person your future wife will ever come second to.

6. The book clearly stresses the need to work on oneself. Should I just stop pursuing women altogether? Is that really going to increase my chances of finding a wife?

I'm not saying that you shouldn't pursue women at all. I think it's good and necessary to pursue a woman who catches your eye. Let it be known you have an interest in her, but do not become consumed with the process. Ultimately, don't let your relationships make you forget about the things you need to focus on in your own life.

The key is to find a good balance, and you want to make sure there is mutual effort being put in at all times. Sometimes it takes a second for her to warm up to your advances. If you're really interested in her, be friends in the meantime (while still being honest about your romantic interest) this is the best option.

Again, still continue to work on you, and this will help increase your chances of getting her interested.

7. **If I have done everything in the book, and still haven't found my wife, then what?**

Stay positive and keep working on you. I know that's easier said than done, but that is really what you have to do. The reality is that we may think we've done everything, yet there are still some things that have been left undone. Also, remember that God's timing is best. He may know that a few things need to be in place first before you are ready to be blessed with a wife.

Go to God again in prayer and ask for clarity and direction on how to proceed and direction on what else you need to do. Don't get discouraged and lose hope because your time will come. Continue to do what you're supposed to do, and you will receive all that you're supposed to have.

12 WAYS TO TURN A WOMAN ON... WITH NO PHYSICAL CONTACT

Do you want to know how to be absolutely irresistible to women? You have to start by learning how to turn a woman on and attract her the right way. What I'm about to share are 12 effective ways to peak a woman's interest, and possibly arouse her in the process. No, this isn't about where to kiss her, and different ways to touch her body. You will be able to achieve great results without ever laying a finger on her.

Non-physical qualities play a big role in generating attraction from a woman and using these can truly make you stand out from the pack.

A SMART MAN IS A SEXY MAN

A lot of women will agree that a smart man is a sexy man. Knowledge is power, and it can definitely be used to intrigue women. Now you might be thinking, "Nerds don't get girls." Well, think again because they do. Having the ability to carry on an intelligent conversation is very attractive and has a very positive effect on a woman. Not to mention it allows you to attract a higher caliber woman because it shows you are very capable of achieving more in life.

So, definitely strive to gain more knowledge. You don't have to go back to school either. There are other ways to educate yourself such as; reading books, going online and watching educational videos, listening to audio seminars on topics you're interested in, and engaging in intelligent discussions with others who share the same interest. Doing so will help you further yourself in life and in your relationships.

LEARN HOW TO BE CONSIDERATE

When you do things that show consideration in your relationship this makes your woman feel special because it shows you care about her and her needs. This is a feeling you should seek to create consistently for your woman because it will materialize into a greater attraction.

Being mindful of her feelings and doing small gestures to show her you're thinking about her can easily win you the kind of points that last. Pouring into her emotionally makes her much more receptive to you. Bring back chivalry and strive to be a gentleman. I know it may seem that a lot of women don't value that enough anymore, but many still do and for the ones who do, this will make you stand out.

KNOW WHEN TO BE ASSERTIVE

Most women (if not all) are turned off by a man they view as too soft or too passive. Knowing when to be assertive and putting your foot down at the right time (in the right way) can cause a woman to melt right before your eyes. This doesn't mean be disrespectful, behave rudely, or treat her like she is beneath you.

Being assertive means that you take action when needed, you communicate with love and with resolution in mind. It also means you stand firm in your beliefs, you handle your business, and you lead by example.

LOOK THE PART

Even though men tend to be more superficial than women, don't be fooled. She is paying attention to everything, and she too wants something nice to look at. You don't need to have expensive clothes or flashy jewelry. Simply, learn how to present yourself as a man who is well put together and see it do wonders. Know how to rock a suit, and that casual outfit. Don't forget a nice pair of shoes (a lot of women are looking at your shoes whether you realize it or not). Wear clothes that compliment you and are well maintained. A good thing to do is go shopping with a woman (friend, acquaintance, sister). They probably know what looks good on you better than you do.

SHOW AMBITION

A man with no aspirations and no drive is a huge turn off for most women. Sure, there are good-for-nothing men who get women, but this is the result of a deeper issue on the part of the woman and a different level of dysfunction that needs to be addressed by her.

The reality is most women crave an ambitious man. Having passion and a purpose can really do it for her. When you can articulate a plan for the road ahead, it gives off the energy of a man who is on top of things and is about handling his business. A woman loves to see that, and it is a huge turn on for her.

KNOW HOW TO GET YOUR HANDS DIRTY

This one isn't a huge issue for a lot of women, but that doesn't mean they don't like to see a man that knows how to get his hands dirty. You don't need to be an all-out mechanic, or build furniture from scratch, but knowing how to fix things around the house, on your own, is a very sexy attribute to a lot of women. It comes off very manly and naturally women are drawn to this masculine energy.

So, take some time to learn how to take care of a few simple tasks. It works to your advantage with women, and it will also help out your pockets by saving you money over time.

BRING ON THE FUNNY

Knowing how to make a woman laugh can take you a long way. Unlike some of the other things mentioned on this list, it probably won't generate much on the "arousal" side of things, but it will definitely draw a woman to you. We all like to smile, so having a good sense of humor is a great thing to have. You don't have to be standup comic funny, and have jokes ready to go on the fly, just remember that laughter is good for the soul, and can definitely help you appear more attractive to a woman.

SHOW HER YOU WANT HER

A woman likes to be respectfully desired. Learning the right ways to show your desire for her will work in your favor. For example, some women love to receive "good morning" texts. Others may want you to initiate seeing them more often, and actually taking them out. Simply giving her a random call because you want to hear her voice can make her feel very special. There are many ways to do it, but you have to try different things and then discuss with her what she enjoys. This will help you get on the right track with showing her the desire she would like to see from you.

SEDUCE HER MENTALLY

Your words and knowing how to use them can be powerful. The ability to communicate effectively will make you a very desirable man. This is how some men who might lack other things on the list still get women. They've learned how to listen (which is a part of communicating) and how to seduce a woman's mind with effective communication. A lot of women love to talk and a man that knows how to talk to them and speak a woman's language will benefit from this. Mental seduction is a main key to success with women, so you definitely want to get better with it.

EXERCISE GOOD HYGIENE

Women in general are sensitive to smell, so if your breath or body is a little funky, then that isn't going to work in your favor. Paying more attention to your hygiene is important to attracting women. Men tend to take this for granted. However, when you smell fresh and clean this makes a woman want to get closer to you. Invest in some good cologne (please don't drown yourself in it), or some other type of smell good that you can use on a daily basis, so that you have a signature scent. Some women may like "funk," but most are turned on by a good smelling man.

EXUDE CONFIDENCE

A man's confidence is one of the most important, if not the most important factor in turning on a woman and getting her attention. Confidence is sexy and women love it! If you lack confidence your energy isn't likely to arouse her one bit. You have to see value in yourself and be comfortable with who you are first. However, don't confuse confidence with arrogance. Confidence presents itself more subtly; arrogance tends to have to announce itself with a bull horn and this in most cases is a turn off.

DEVELOP A PERSONAL RELATIONSHIP WITH GOD

Believe it or not, your relationship with God is a huge turn on for many women. Of course, that isn't the main reason to have one, but it still does make an impact. The fact that you show an ability to commit, be disciplined, and strive to improve yourself contributes to your allure. There are other reasons that play into this as well. The simple fact is, a lot of women are drawn to a man who embraces a life of walking with God.

SUMMARY

You may read this and say you've seen plenty of men get women doing much less. As I stated earlier that is a different issue, and that still doesn't dismiss the fact that practicing the action items on this list can indeed turn a lot of women on and increase your chances of finding a woman you're crazy about and who in turn is crazy about you. The items listed here are good habits for a man to implement in his life that will be beneficial for him with more than just women.

Before you disregard them as too much work, try them out and see for yourself.

● ● ● ●

ABOUT THE AUTHOR

Stephan Labossiere is *the* "Relationship Guy." An authority on real love, real talk, real relationships. The brand *Stephan Speaks* is synonymous with happier relationships and healthier people around the globe. For more than a decade, Stephan has committed himself to breaking down relationship barriers, pushing past common facades, and exposing the truth. It is his understanding of REAL relationships that has empowered millions of people, clients and readers alike, to create their best lives by being able to experience and sustain greater love.

Seen, heard, and chronicled in national and international media outlets including; the *Tom Joyner Morning Show*, *The Examiner*, *ABC*, *GQ*, and *Huffington Post Live*. The certified life & relationship coach, speaker, and award winning, bestselling author is the voice that the world tunes into for answers to their difficult relationship woes. From understanding the opposite sex, to navigating the paths and avoiding the pitfalls of relationships and self-growth, Stephan's relationship advice and insight helps countless men and women overcome the situations hindering them from achieving an authentically amazing life.

Stephan is highly sought-after because he is able to dispel the myths of relationship breakdowns and obstacles–platonic, romantic, and otherwise—with fervor and finesse. His signature style, relatability, and passion make international audiences sit up and pay attention.

"My message is simple: life and relationships require truth. The willingness to speak truth and the bravery to acknowledge truth is paramount."

Are you listening?

Enough said.

Coming Soon By
STEPHAN SPEAKS

www.HealingHeartbreakBook.com

Printed in Great Britain
by Amazon